D0764031

21st Century Skills **INNOVATION** *Library*

From African Plant to ...
Vaccine Preservative

by Nel Yomtov

CHERRY
LAKE
Publishing

Published in the United States of America by Cherry Lake Publishing
Ann Arbor, Michigan
www.cherrylakepublishing.com

Content Adviser: Marjan Eggermont, Senior Instructor, Schulich School of Engineering, Calgary,
Alberta, Canada

Reading Adviser: Marla Conn, ReadAbility, Inc.

Design: The Design Lab

Photo Credits: Cover and page 3, ©Nixx Photography/Shutterstock, Inc.; cover inset, ©Emilio Ereza/Alamy; page 4,
©iStockphoto.com/PhotoEuphoria; page 6, ©Classic Image/Alamy; page 7, ©Art Directors & TRIP/Alamy; pages 9
and 10, ©blickwinkel/Alamy; page 13, ©iStockphoto.com/JanekWD; page 14, ©Skynavin/Shutterstock, Inc.; page
15, ©Blend Images/Alamy; page 16, ©Canadian Press via AP Images; page 17, ©Michael Rosenfeld/picture-alliance/
dpa/AP Images; pages 18 and 27, ©AP Photo/John D McHugh; page 20, ©PRNewsFoto/Minnesota Thermal Science;
page 21, ©Adam Ziaja/Shutterstock, Inc.; page 23, ©Ilike/Shutterstock, Inc.; page 24, ©PHOVOIR/Alamy; page 25,
©Monkey Business Images/Shutterstock, Inc.; page 28, ©Ugo Cei/Alamy; page 29, ©The Print Collector/Alamy.

Library of Congress Cataloging-in-Publication Data
Yomtov, Nel.
 From African plant to vaccine preservative / by Nel Yomtov.
    pages cm. – (Innovations from Nature)
 Includes bibliographical references and index.
 ISBN 978-1-62431-753-8 (lib. bdg.) – ISBN 978-1-62431-765-1 (pdf) –
ISBN 978-1-62431-759-0 (pbk.) – ISBN 978-1-62431-771-2 (e-book)
 1. Vaccines–Juvenile literature. 2. Drugs–Preservation–Juvenile literature.
3. Desert plants–Juvenile literature. 4. Biomimicry–Juvenile literature. I. Title.
 RM281.Y66 2014
 615.3'72–dc23   2013030376

Cherry Lake Publishing would like to acknowledge the work of
The Partnership for 21st Century Skills.
Please visit www.p21.org *for more information.*

Printed in the United States of America
Corporate Graphics Inc.
January 2014

CONTENTS

Keeping You Healthy

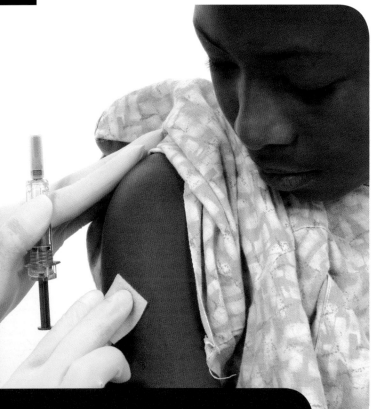

Shots aren't fun, but they are an important part of staying healthy.

Nobody likes getting shots. They can hurt, and the sight of getting jabbed with a sharp needle can be scary. However, shots keep us healthy. Some of the shots we get are called **vaccinations**. Vaccinations prevent us from getting serious diseases that can make us very ill or even die. When you think about it, the sting of a shot isn't nearly as bad as those diseases.

Our bodies get sick when germs, such as **viruses** and some **bacteria**, invade them. When the measles virus enters your body, it gives you measles. Tetanus bacteria cause tetanus, a disease of the muscles. When germs enter your body, they begin to multiply. Your body recognizes these invading germs and makes substances called **antibodies** to fight them. The germs have a head start, though! By the time your body produces enough antibodies to destroy them, you will probably be sick already.

The antibodies have two jobs. First, they help destroy the attacking germs. Then they remain in your body to guard against future infections. If the same germs try to infect you again, even after many years, the antibodies will protect you. This time, they can destroy the germs before you get sick.

The part of your body that makes antibodies and fights infections is called the **immune system**. The only problem with this system is that you have to get sick before you develop a protection against specific germs. That's where vaccinations come in.

Vaccinations give you protection from a disease before it can make you sick. They contain a type of medicine called a vaccine. Vaccines are made from the same germ that causes the disease. For example, the measles vaccine is made from the measles virus. The germs in vaccines are either dead or weakened so they won't make you sick.

When you get a shot of a vaccine, your immune system behaves as if the real disease were invading. It reacts by making antibodies. The antibodies destroy the vaccine germs, just like they would kill real disease germs. Then they stay in your system to protect you in the future.

Vaccines have been amazingly successful at preventing diseases throughout the world. A disease called smallpox once killed millions of people every year. By 1979, it was almost totally wiped out, thanks to an international vaccination program. In 1988, the World Health Organization (WHO) launched a program to eliminate the disease known as polio. Today, the number

The smallpox vaccine was discovered in 1796 by English surgeon Edward Jenner.

of polio infections around the world has decreased by 99 percent. Dozens of other diseases, including whooping cough, meningitis, and rubella, are now distant memories because of vaccines.

Yet even when a vaccine has been developed, not everyone has access to it. Hundreds of thousands of people die each year because they have not been vaccinated. This often occurs because the vaccines cannot be properly preserved. Vaccines are often made thousands of miles away from the people who need them. Most vaccines that contain disease germs must be kept cold. If they get too warm,

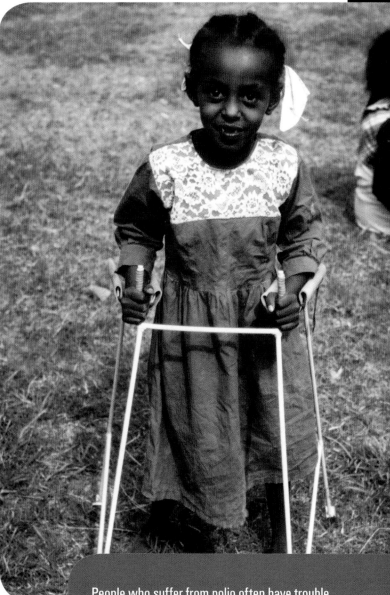

People who suffer from polio often have trouble walking because they cannot move their legs.

21st Century Content

 Most vaccines are injected into your body with a needle. You may have wondered why this is so. The answer is because a vaccine injected with a needle can get into your blood quickly. This is where it needs to be for your body to recognize it and begin making antibodies. If you swallowed the vaccine, it would go through your stomach first. The chemicals in your stomach would prevent the vaccine from making protective antibodies. Also, not enough of the vaccine would get into your blood.

The pain you feel when getting a shot is like a small sting. The spot where you get the injection may become sore or tender after a few hours. However, this is a small price to pay for staying free of deadly diseases.

they will stop working correctly. This means the vaccines must be kept in refrigerators or freezers.

That can sometimes be tricky. In some parts of the world, there is no electricity available to refrigerate the vaccines. Scientists have developed ways of keeping vaccines cold as they are shipped around the world. These systems are not perfect, though. Millions of people still do not get vaccinated.

Scientists face a serious problem. How do they get lifesaving vaccines to people in remote areas? They need a method to store and preserve vaccines for long periods of time without refrigeration. Amazingly, scientists are finding the solution in an unexpected place—the plant kingdom.

CHAPTER TWO

A Remarkable Desert Plant

The resurrection plant is one of nature's hardiest forms of life. It grows in dry, desert regions such as Texas and Arizona. It is found in Central and South America and throughout southern Africa. Growing up to 1 foot (0.3 meters) tall, the plant looks like a cross between moss and ferns. It has no flowers,

Resurrection plants are able to survive in very dry environments.

The resurrection plant dries up and turns brown when it doesn't have enough water, but it does not die.

fruits, or seeds. Its "leaves" are actually leaflike growths of the stem.

The resurrection plant may not be much to look at, but it has conquered its harsh environment as few other plants have. It grows in cracks in rocks or in dry soil, baking under the hot desert sun. Its neighbors are cacti and other desert plants. Under these rugged conditions, the resurrection plant has developed a remarkable way to survive.

Rain rarely falls in the regions where the resurrection plant grows. When the soil is moist after a rainfall, a resurrection plant absorbs water from the ground with its roots and grows quickly. But the plant is unable to store water for later. As the soil dries, the resurrection plant folds its stems into a tight ball and begins to dry up. It appears to be dead.

The plant isn't dead, though. Instead, it remains in a "sleeping" state for months or even years. When the plant finally comes into contact with water, it jumps right back to life! The stem unfolds, and the plant begins to grow again. If the **cells** in human bodies were to dry out, they would shrink, shrivel up, and become badly damaged.

What's the secret of the resurrection plant's stunning ability to return from the "dead"? A University of California–Davis biologist named John Crowe discovered the answer. In the late 1970s, Crowe found that resurrection plants manufacture a sugar called **trehalose** as they dry out. The sugar acts just like water inside the plant's cells.

As the cells dry up, trehalose slips into the spaces where water used to be. The sugar **bonds** with the cells

21st Century Content

The resurrection plant belongs to a group of plants known as lycopods. Lycopods are commonly called ground pines or club mosses. They are among the oldest living plants on Earth. The first lycopods appeared at least 400 million years ago. These ancient lycopods looked very different from the ones living today. Between 345 million and 280 million years ago, they grew as giant trees. Many were more than 100 feet (30 m) tall, with trunks 6 feet (1.8 m) around. These huge trees were found mostly in swampy areas. These giant lycopods eventually died out. However, smaller relatives such as the resurrection plant survive to this day.

and prevents them from shriveling. It also keeps the contents of the cells from moving around or joining together. These things could damage or destroy the cells.

Crowe began to wonder if trehalose could be used to protect human cells when they were dried. He decided to experiment on human blood **platelets**. These are cells in our bloodstream that join together to form clots that stop bleeding. Platelets also make substances to help wounds heal. Patients whose platelets don't function properly are given blood **transfusions**. These transfusions contain healthy platelets. The platelets have to be stored at room temperature, though. They are thrown out after five days because they could become spoiled.

Crowe placed healthy platelets in a bath of trehalose. The platelets absorbed the sugar. Then Crowe exposed the platelets to extremely cold temperatures. This turned them into a dried powder. When Crowe added water to the powder, the platelets sprang back to life. They were healthy and able to form clots. Crowe's dried platelets can be stored at room temperature for two years. That is plenty of time to get them to people with blood illnesses.

Crowe's discovery was based on the concept of **biomimicry**. In plain language, biomimicry is the practice of copying nature to improve humans' lives. His work gave other researchers an idea: Can sugars like the ones produced by the resurrection plant be used to preserve vaccines?

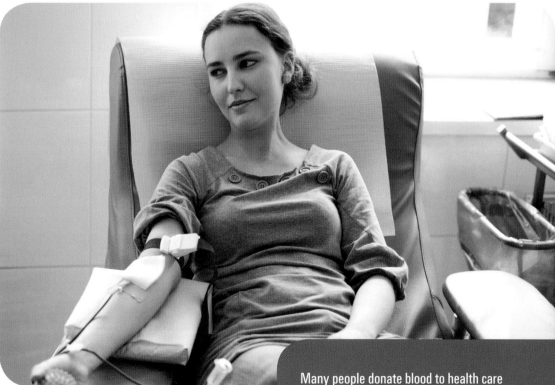

Many people donate blood to health care organizations so it can be used for transfusions.

CHAPTER THREE

How It's Done

Vaccines must be in a liquid form before they can be injected.

Motivated by John Crowe's breakthrough, researchers have been working on creating dried vaccines that do not need to be refrigerated. A British company called Cambridge Biostability Limited (CBL) is one of the leading research firms involved in this quest.

Led by Dr. Bruce Roser, CBL scientists sprayed a vaccine with a mixture of sugar and water. They then dried the vaccine mixture using hot gases. As the vaccine dried, it turned into a thick syrup. As more water was removed, it solidified into a glass-like state. The vaccine remains safe in this state. It can survive extreme temperatures without refrigeration.

The dry vaccine is then put into a special type of liquid. This liquid has no effect on the vaccine. When the vaccine is ready to be used, it is injected into a patient. The "glass" softens when it comes into contact with bodily fluids. The vaccine is released and comes back to life in the patient's body!

"If it takes off on a large scale, this is a revolutionary development," says Roser. "So many of the world's children are not immunized [vaccinated]—not because

A vacccine that has been preserved using Dr. Bruce Roser's method becomes active when it mixes with a patient's blood.

the vaccines are not available, but because it is so expensive to transport and store them."

The process of keeping vaccines at low temperatures from the time they are made until the time they are used costs WHO about $250 million per year. This is money that could be spent on more vaccinations. Experts say that removing the need to refrigerate vaccines could

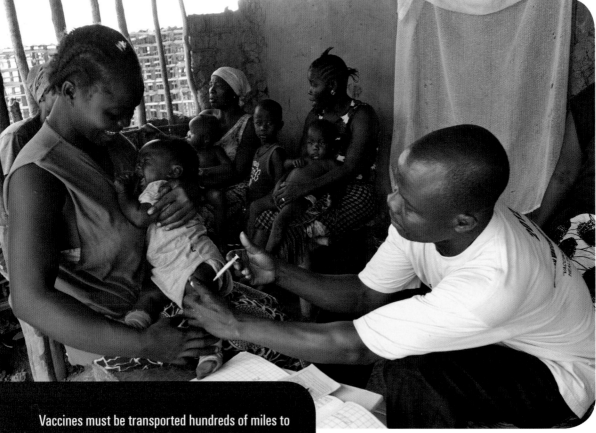

Vaccines must be transported hundreds of miles to reach people who live far from major cities.

Vaccines must be handled carefully to keep them from being ruined during transport.

save enough money to vaccinate another 10 million children.

CBL's research will also prevent losing vaccines because they have frozen. Vaccines are packed in boxes that use cold blocks to keep the temperature down. The blocks must warm up a bit before they are put in the boxes. If this is not done, the blocks will freeze the vials of vaccine that come near them. WHO says about

Preservation methods based on the resurrection plant could greatly increase the amount of vaccine that reaches remote locations.

70 percent of all the vaccines delivered to local clinics around the world are lost due to freezing.

Being exposed to temperatures that are too warm or too cold is not the only reason more than half of all the vaccines manufactured each year are ruined. Other causes include not using the vaccine before its expiration date, breaking or losing vials of vaccine, and using dirty needles that introduce germs into the vials.

Hilary Benn, England's one-time secretary of state for international development, has said, "We want to make this a reality for children and their parents in the developing world. This new British technology allows vaccines to be used in remote areas and at extreme temperatures, and will mean more children than ever before will have access to life-saving vaccinations."

Learning & Innovation Skills

 The American Academy of Pediatrics (AAP) recommends that children who are at least six months old get an influenza, or flu, vaccine each year. The flu is an infection that affects the breathing system. It can be very serious and even life threatening. The vaccine is usually given as a shot in the muscle or under the skin. In some cases, it can be given as a nose spray. The Mayo Clinic, a worldwide leader in medical care, also recommends a Tdap vaccine. This is a combination vaccine to prevent tetanus, diphtheria, and pertussis. Tetanus affects the nervous system and muscles, diphtheria is a breathing disease, and pertussis is commonly known as whooping cough.

CHAPTER FOUR

A Sweet Future

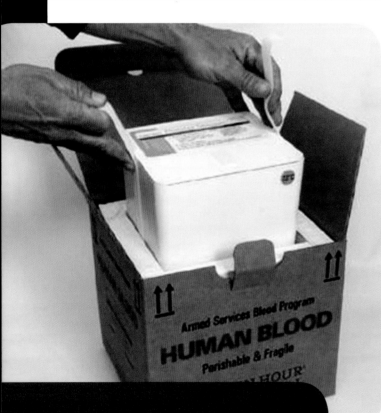

Like vaccines, blood used for transfusions is fragile and difficult to transport.

John Crowe's success using trehalose to freeze-dry platelets has raised many interesting possibilities. Realizing this, the U.S. Department of Defense funded much of Crowe's research. Platelets are usually unavailable to soldiers on the battlefield because it is difficult to store them safely for long periods of time. The Defense Department hopes that there will be more

John Crowe's preservation methods might one day save the lives of soldiers who are traveling far from medical facilities.

research on preserving platelets. Crowe believes it might be possible that every soldier going into combat will one day have a little packet of platelets and blood cells in his or her backpack.

Learning & Innovation Skills

Trehalose itself has many health benefits. It is found in honey, shrimp, and varieties of cacti and mushrooms. Trehalose has 45 percent of the sweetness of common sugar, but it lacks the harmful effects of sugar, such as weight gain. People can double up on portions of trehalose when using it in cooking. There is also evidence that it reduces cravings for food and sweets. Some research has even shown that trehalose is effective at helping people with nervous system disorders. Improvements in muscle control have been observed in several studies of nerve diseases.

The future of vaccines that do not have to be refrigerated is also bright. Researchers believe that trehalose technology might eliminate the need for booster shots of a vaccine. A booster shot is an extra dose of a vaccine given years after an earlier dose. It is given to increase the body's protection after the original vaccine has weakened over time. Scientists can tweak the "glass" of the trehalose and vaccine solution to dissolve at different times when it is in the body. This means a shot you get today can continue providing your body with fresh vaccine for years.

Also on the drawing board is a single vaccine for several major childhood diseases targeted by WHO. Such a vaccine could save the lives of millions of people, especially babies and young children. About 132 million children are born worldwide each year. More than one-quarter, or

Eliminating the need for booster shots would allow people to stay healthy while getting fewer shots.

34 million, do not receive vaccinations. Imagine a single vaccine that could eliminate diseases such as measles, tetanus, and polio!

Although more research is needed to determine other benefits and potential uses of trehalose, it's amazing how many have already been found for this simple sugar provided by nature.

Scientists may one day develop a single shot that contains everything your body needs to fight off many common diseases.

CHAPTER FIVE

Vaccine Visionaries

Several creative thinkers have made important contributions to the worlds of vaccine preservation and biomimicry.

Dr. John Crowe (1943–) is a professor of cellular and molecular biology at the University of California–Davis. He discovered that resurrection plants are able to thrive in dry desert climates by making trehalose. Using what he observed,

Cellular and molecular biologists study the smallest parts of living things.

Life & Career Skills

Biologists will play a key role in the future of biomimicry. A cellular biologist is someone who studies the cellular structure of organisms. Some biologists study single-celled organisms, especially those associated with diseases or environmental problems. Other cellular biologists study the structures of larger plants and animals. To become a cellular biologist, start planning early. In high school, take advanced courses in science and math. In college, you'll study for a degree in cell biology. You'll take courses such as chemistry, genetics, and cellular biology.

he pioneered a process of drying human blood platelets. His work led the way for the study of trehalose in vaccine preservation.

Dr. Bruce Roser (1935–) is currently director of StablePharma, a biotechnology company in England. From 1998 to 2009, he served as director and chief scientific adviser at Cambridge Biostability. While there, he invented the technique for drying vaccines using trehalose. He is a graduate of the University of Sydney in Australia.

Leonardo da Vinci (1452–1519) the painter of the *Mona Lisa*, was also a sculptor, engineer, mathematician, musician, mapmaker, and inventor. He believed that many of humankind's problems could be solved through careful study of plants and animals. His sketches of machines that he believed could fly—early versions of today's modern aircraft—were based on his study of birds. Da Vinci was one of the first

Dr. Bruce Roser's work could one day save millions of lives.

scientists to recognize the science of underwater sound, which has been used by sea creatures for millions of years. In 1490, he wrote, "If you cause your ship to stop and place the head of a long tube in the water and place the outer extremity to your ear, you will hear ships at a great distance from you."

The inspiration provided by the resurrection plant is just one of many examples of biomimicry at work.

Leonardo da Vinci is best remembered as an artist, but he was also a pioneer of biomimicry.

Glossary

antibodies (AN-ti-bah-deez) substances your body makes to fight infections and diseases

bacteria (bak-TEER-ee-uh) tiny, single-celled living things that can either be harmful or useful

biomimicry (bye-oh-MI-mi-kree) the practice of studying and copying nature's forms and systems to solve human problems

bonds (BAHNDZ) forms a physical connection between cells

cells (SELZ) the smallest units of animals or plants

immune system (i-MYOON SIS-tuhm) the system that protects your body against disease and infection

platelets (PLATE-lits) disk-shaped bodies in the blood that form clots to prevent bleeding

transfusions (trans-FYOO-zhuhnz) injections of blood from one person into the body of someone else who is sick or injured

trehalose (trih-HAH-loess) a sugar created by the resurrection plant

vaccinations (vak-suh-NAY-shuhnz) shots given to protect people against a disease

viruses (VYE-ruh-siz) tiny organisms that can cause disease

For More Information

BOOKS

Gates, Phil. *Nature Got There First*. New York: Kingfisher, 2010.

Lee, Dora. *Biomimicry: Inventions Inspired by Nature*. Tonawanda, NY: Kids Can Press, 2011.

WEB SITES

Ask Nature: What Is Biomimicry?
www.asknature.org/article/view/what_is_biomimicry
Find out more about biomimicry with examples, links, and interesting video content.

Biomimicry 3.8
www.biomimicry.net
Check out the latest news on the science of biomimicry, with links to other sites as well as information for those interested in choosing a career in the field.

Index

About the Author

Nel Yomtov is an award-winning author of nonfiction books and graphic novels for young readers. He lives in the New York City area.